2-11

Murray, Julie.
Erie Canal

84D18
3.2
0.2

ALL ABOARD AMERICA

Erie Canal

A Buddy Book
by
Julie Murray

ABDO
Publishing Company

VISIT US AT
www.abdopub.com

Published by ABDO Publishing Company, 4940 Viking Drive, Edina, Minnesota 55435.

Printed in the United States.

Edited by: Christy DeVillier
Contributing Editors: Michael P. Goecke, Sarah Tieck
Graphic Design: Deborah Coldiron
Image Research: Deborah Coldiron
Photographs: Corbis, Digital Vision, Erie Canal Museum, Hulton Archives, Library of Congress, North Wind Pictures

Library of Congress Cataloging-in-Publication Data

Murray, Julie, 1969-
  Erie Canal / Julie Murray.
      p. cm. — (All aboard America)
  Includes bibliographical references (p.) and index.
  ISBN 1-59197-504-2
    1. Erie Canal (N.Y.)—History—Juvenile literature. I. Title.

F127.E5M87 2005
974.7'96—dc22

                                                    2004046274

Table of Contents

Famous Waterway .4

The Idea 6

DeWitt Clinton 8

The Work 10

Celebrating The Erie Canal 14

Success 16

The Erie Canal Today 20

Important Words .22

Web Sites 23

Index 24

CHAPTER 1

Famous Waterway

The Erie Canal is a famous man-made waterway. It is in the state of New York. The canal went from Buffalo to Troy. This waterway joined Lake Erie and the Hudson River. It linked the Great Lakes to the Atlantic Ocean.

It took eight years to build the Erie Canal. The total building cost was more than $7 million.

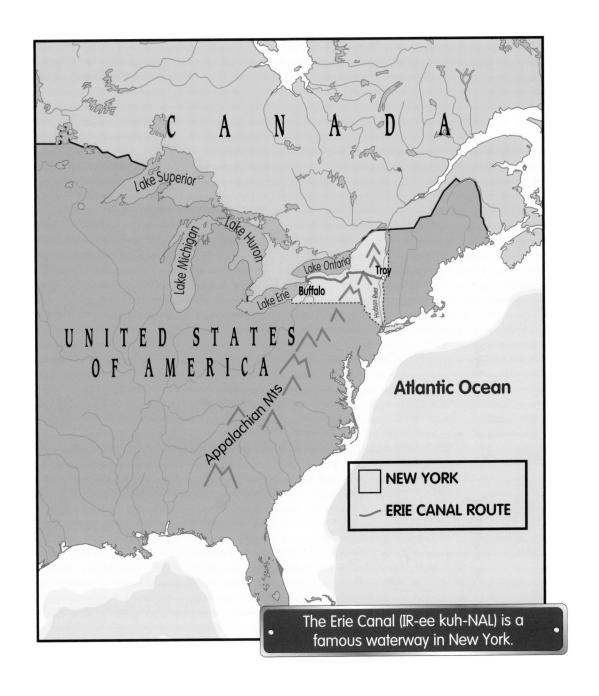

CANADA

Lake Superior

Lake Michigan

Lake Huron

Lake Ontario

Lake Erie

UNITED STATES
OF AMERICA

Troy

Buffalo

Hudson River

Appalachian Mts

Atlantic Ocean

☐ **NEW YORK**

⌒ **ERIE CANAL ROUTE**

The Erie Canal (IR-ee kuh-NAL) is a famous waterway in New York.

In the late 1700s and early 1800s, many American settlers wanted to move West. But crossing the Appalachian Mountains was not easy. The Appalachians stretch from Canada to Alabama.

People talked about building a canal. It would be a safe way to cross the Appalachians. Cadwallader Colden thought a canal joining Lake Erie and the Hudson River would work. Colden was a **land surveyor** in New York. He brought up his canal idea in 1724.

Many Americans wanted to begin a new life in the West.

DeWitt Clinton was the mayor of New York, New York, in the early 1800s. He believed building a canal was a good idea. Clinton began collecting money for the project. Not everyone thought the canal was a good idea. Some people called it "Clinton's ditch."

Clinton won much support for the canal. In 1817, the state of New York agreed to the project. The state set aside money to build the canal.

DeWitt Clinton became the governor of New York in 1817.

Famous engineer John B. Jervis worked on the Erie Canal.

CHAPTER 4

The Work

People began building the Erie Canal on July 4, 1817. Workers began digging the canal in Rome, New York. They cut down trees and hauled away dirt. Workers also built a pathway next to the canal. This pathway was for horses and mules. These animals would pull boats down the canal.

Horses and mules pulled boats down the Erie Canal.

Did You Know?

The Erie Canal workers were farmers and Irish immigrants. They had no training in building a canal. Their tools were picks, shovels, and wheelbarrows. It was a tough job. They worked more than 14 hours each day. Workers earned about 80¢ each day.

Cutting down trees was slow work. Some workers made a special machine to help them. It was a stump puller. Workers used it to remove tree stumps from the ground.

In the summer of 1819, the Erie Canal reached the Montezuma Swamp. There were many mosquitoes. Workers suffered from mosquito bites. Many caught **malaria** and died.

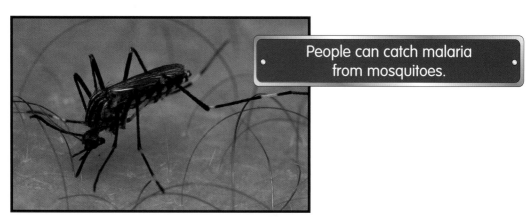

People can catch malaria from mosquitoes.

Locks helped boats travel up and down the Erie Canal.

Lake Erie was more than 500 feet (152 m) higher than the Hudson River. Workers needed to build **locks**. A lock system helps boats travel different levels of a waterway. Workers also built bridges over rivers and streams.

The Erie Canal was finished in 1825. It was 363 miles (584 km) long. DeWitt Clinton rode the first boat down the Erie Canal. This boat was called the *Seneca Chief*. Crowds gathered to watch the *Seneca Chief*. Towns along the Erie Canal celebrated.

The *Seneca Chief* reached New York City's harbor on November 4. DeWitt Clinton poured water from Lake Erie into the Atlantic Ocean. People called it the "wedding of the waters."

People cheered as the *Seneca Chief* traveled down the Erie Canal.

CHAPTER 6

Success

The Erie Canal was a huge success. It was an important trade route. Shipping goods on the canal was fast and cheap. The Erie Canal allowed more trade than ever before.

Many people used the canal to move West. They rode on packet boats. A trip down the whole canal took between three and seven days.

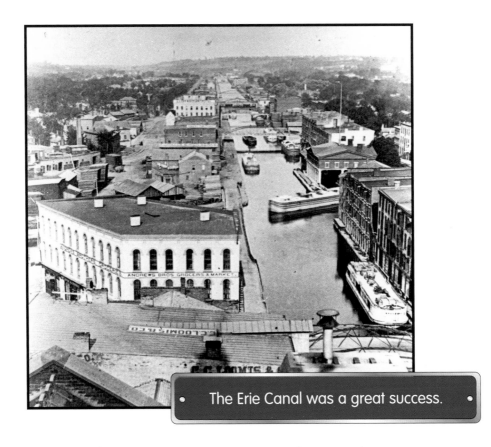

The Erie Canal was a great success.

Over the years, towns along the canal grew. Utica, Rochester, Syracuse, and Buffalo became important cities. By 1840, New York City was the nation's busiest port.

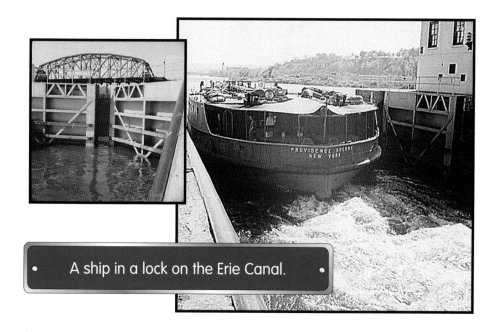

A ship in a lock on the Erie Canal.

The Erie Canal was very busy. In 1836, people began working to widen and deepen the canal. This allowed bigger boats to use it.

Many railroads were built in the 1850s. The railroad was a faster way to ship goods across the country. Fewer people used the Erie Canal after 1865.

Steam trains took business away from the Erie Canal.

In 1903, the state of New York decided to join four canals together. The Erie Canal became part of the New York State **Barge** Canal System. This canal system opened in 1918.

Today the Erie Canal is part of the Erie Canalway National Heritage Corridor. The Erie Canalway includes the Champlain, Oswego, and Cayuga-Seneca canals. It covers 524 miles (843 km) throughout upstate New York.

Parks along the Erie Canal offer trails for visitors to use.

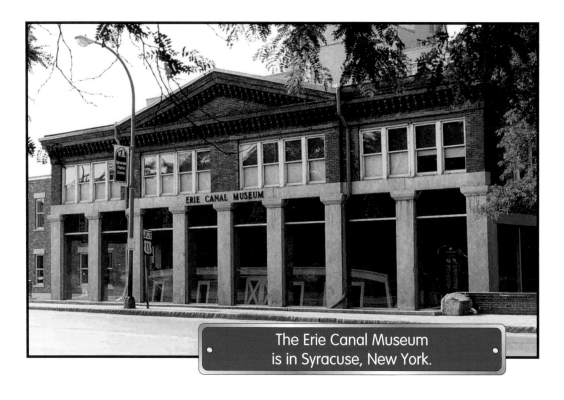

The Erie Canal Museum
is in Syracuse, New York.

Many people use the Erie Canalway for **recreation**. They go there for fishing and canoeing. There are trails along the canal for hiking and biking. Boat cruises are common, too.

barge (BARJ) a large boat with a flat bottom.

immigrant (IH-muh-grent) someone who has left their home and settled in a new country.

land surveyor (LAND suhr-VAY-uhr) someone who measures land.

lock (LAHK) part of a canal or river that is closed off with gates on each end. The lock uses water to raise or lower boats.

malaria (muh-LAIR-ee-uh) a deadly disease carried by mosquitoes.

recreation (reh-kree-AY-shun) activities that refresh a person's mind and body after work.

Web Sites

Would you like to learn more about
the Erie Canal?

Please visit ABDO Publishing Company on the
information superhighway to find Web site links about
the Erie Canal. These links are routinely
monitored and updated to provide the most current
information available.

www.abdopub.com

Index

Alabama **6**

Appalachian Mountains **5, 6**

Atlantic Ocean **4, 5, 14**

Buffalo, NY **4, 5, 17**

Canada **5, 6**

Cayuga-Seneca Canal **20**

Champlain Canal **20**

"Clinton's ditch" **8**

Clinton, DeWitt **8, 9, 14**

Colden, Cadwallader **6**

Erie Canalway National Heritage
Corridor **20, 21**

Erie, Lake **4, 5, 6, 13, 14**

Great Lakes **4, 5**

Hudson River **4, 5, 6, 13**

immigrants **11**

locks **13, 18**

malaria **12**

Montezuma Swamp **12**

mosquitoes **12**

mules **10**

New York **4, 5, 6, 8, 9, 19, 20**

New York, NY **8, 14, 17**

New York State Barge Canal
System **19**

Oswego Canal **20**

railroads **18, 19**

Rochester, NY **17**

Rome, NY **10**

Seneca Chief **14, 15**

settlers **6, 7**

Syracuse, NY **17, 21**

Troy, NY **4, 5**

Utica, NY **17**

"wedding of the waters" **14**